Venus Flytraps, Bladderworts, and Other Wild and Amazing Plants

Venus
Flytraps,
Bladderworts,
and
Other Wild and Amazing
Plants

By Monica Halpern

NATIONAL GEOGRAPHIC

WASHINGTON D.C.

One of the world's largest nonprofit scientific and educational organizations, the National Geographic Society was founded in 1888 "for the increase and diffusion of geographic knowledge." Fulfilling this mission, the Society educates and inspires millions every day through its magazines, books, television programs, videos, maps and atlases, research grants, the National Geographic Bee, teacher workshops, and innovative classroom materials. The Society is supported through membership dues, charitable gifts, and income from the sale of its educational products. This support is vital to National Geographic's mission to increase global understanding and promote conservation of our planet through exploration, research, and education.

For more information, please call
1-800-NGS-LINE (647-5463) or write to the following address:
National Geographic Society
1145 17th Street N.W.
Washington, D.C. 20036-4688
U.S.A.

For information about special discounts for bulk purchases, please contact
National Geographic Books Special Sales at ngspecsales@ngs.org

Visit the Society's Web site: www.nationalgeographic.com

Published by National Geographic Society. Washington, D.C. 20036

Design by Project Design Company

Printed in the United States

Library of Congress Cataloging-in-Publication Data

Halpern, Monica.
  Venus flytraps, bladderworts, and other wild and amazing plants / by Monica Halpern.
      p. cm. -- (National Geographic science chapters)
  Includes bibliographical references and index.
  ISBN-13: 978-0-7922-5957-2 (library binding)
  ISBN-10: 0-7922-5957-2 (library binding)
1. Carnivorous plants. 2. Poisonous plants. 3. Plant defenses. I. Title. II. Series.
  QK917.H35 2006
  580--dc22

                    2006016336

Photo Credits
Front Cover: © Robert Ross/ Getty Images; Spine: © Mark Daffey/ Lonely Planet Images/ Getty Images; Endpaper: © Mark Daffey/ Lonely Planet Images/ Getty Images; 2-3: © Maryellen Baker/ Botanica/ Picturequest/ Jupiter Images; 6: © Jean-Paul Ferrero/ Auscape; 8: © Colin Monteath/ Auscape; 9 (left): © Erwin & Peggy Bauer/ Auscape; 9 (right): © Jaime Plaza Van Roon; 10, 12: ANT Photo Library; 13: © William Dahl/ Botanical Society of America, 14 (left),15: © ANT Photo Library; 14 (right): © David M. Denis/ Auscape;16, 17: © ANT Photo Library; 18: © Kathie Atkinson/ Oxford Scientific; 19: © Robert F. Sisson/ National Geographic Image Collection; 20-21: © Jean-Paul Ferrero/ Auscape; 22: © Millard H. Sharp/ Photo Researchers, Inc.; 23: © Joel Sartore/ National Geographic/ Getty Images; 24-25: © Paul A. Zahl/ National Geographic Image Collection; 26: © Wally Eberhart/ Botanica/ Picture Quest/ Jupiter Images; 27; © Karen Froment/ Botanica/ Picture Quest/ Jupiter Images; 28: © Photolibrary.com; 29: © Peter Von Balmoos; 30: © Stephern G. St. John/ National Geographic Image Collection; 33: © ANT Photo Library; 34: © Erwin & Peggy Bauer/ Auscape.

Contents

Plants Are Important

Did you know that you couldn't live without plants? Plants provide much of the oxygen that people and other animals breathe. Plants provide much of the food they eat, too.

Plants are living things that can do some amazing things. Most plants make their own food. They grow everywhere. They keep on growing until they die.

Plants come in all sizes and shapes. Some have colorful flowers. Others have no flowers. Some are extremely tall. Others are are so tiny that you need a microscope to see them.

These plants grow in a tropical rain forest.

Lavender and lichens grow in a mountain range in Mongolia.

Plants come in many different colors, shapes, and sizes because they live in many different kinds of places. They live in wet swamps and dry deserts. They live on cold mountaintops and in lush river valleys. They have adapted, or changed, so that they can survive in the places in which they live.

Unlike animals and people, plants can't move around. Most are rooted in one place. But they still need to protect themselves from their enemies. They also have to find a way to get water and minerals, or food.

This tall, spiky cactus grows in dry desert areas.

These giant lilies grow in a forest in Australia.

Many plants have developed interesting ways to find food and to protect themselves. Some produce poisons to keep animals from eating them. Others have sharp thorns that scratch animals that get too close. Still others catch and eat animals! Let's take a look at some of these amazing plants.

Did You Know?

Scientists have discovered more than 350,000 species, or kinds, of plants.

Chapter 1

Meat-Eating Plants

Of the hundreds of thousands of different kinds of plants in our world, only about 400 eat meat. Most of these plants grow in wet places such as swamps, marshes, or bogs. The soil in these places is poor. It doesn't have enough minerals to keep plants healthy. So, these meat-eating plants have adapted over time. They get the minerals they need by eating animals.

Meat-eating plants are too small to eat large animals. Most of them eat insects. But a few eat mice, frogs, and even small birds.

The cobra lily is a meat-eating plant that lives in swamps.

The butterwort plant feeds on insects.

All meat-eating plants do some things in the same ways. They offer a special treat, or bait, to attract animals. They catch the animals in some kind of trap. Then, they dissolve the animals into a kind of soup. Finally, they digest the soup.

Did You Know?

Of all the strange plants, the Venus flytrap is the most popular. People like to have them as houseplants.

Venus Flytraps

One of the best known of the meat-eating plants is the Venus flytrap. This plant lures its victims with a sweet treat. A sugary liquid covers its leaves.

Insects smell the sweet liquid. They crawl onto the leaves, expecting a delicious meal. Instead, tiny hairs on the leaves know the insect is there. These hairs act as triggers. SNAP! The leaves snap shut. The closed leaves form a cage. The insect can't escape.

Venus flytraps grow in bogs in the southeastern United States.

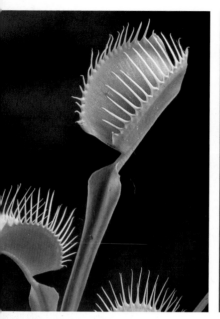

1. The open leaves of a Venus flytrap attract insects.

2. When a fly lands, it triggers the leaves to snap shut.

The sides of the trap start to press together. Within 30 minutes, the insect is squashed and killed. Then, the trap fills with liquid. Over a week or two, most of the insect's body dissolves into a kind of soup. The plant eats its meal. The leaves then open again, ready for the next meal to arrive.

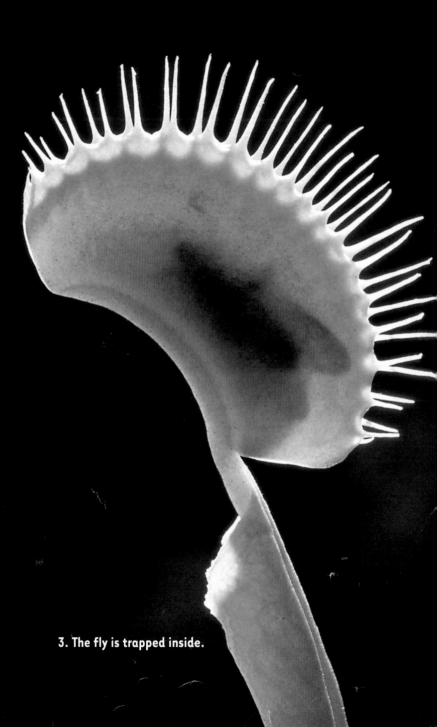

3. The fly is trapped inside.

The bladderwort plant floats in water.

Bladderworts

The tiniest of the meat-eaters is the bladderwort. It may be small, but it can still catch tiny insects. It does this by sucking them up!

Most bladderworts live in water. They float in lakes and ponds. Some bladderworts even live in puddles.

The bladderwort's leaves have what look like tiny bubbles on them. These bubbles are the bladders that catch and digest the victims. Some bladders are so small you need a microscope to see them.

Each bladder has a trapdoor with tiny hairs near it. If an insect touches some of the hairs, the trapdoor suddenly opens. WOOSH! The victim is sucked into the bladder and the trapdoor snaps shut. The animal is trapped. This happens faster than the eye can see.

This bladderwort has captured a tiny water flea.

Pitcher Plants

Unlike bladderworts, pitcher plants have no moving parts. They drown their victims. Some pitcher plants are tiny and catch only small insects. But in some parts of the world, pitcher plants are large enough to catch mice, lizards, or frogs.

The pitcher plant's leaves are shaped like a pitcher. Many are brightly colored, with bright red streaks along the top. The leaves have a sugary liquid along their edges.

When an insect flies by a plant, it sees the colorful pitcher and smells something sweet.

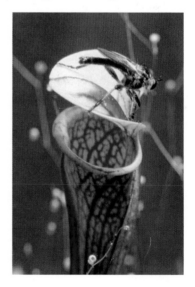

The leaves of a pitcher plant form a pitcher shape with steep sides.

A spider crawls along the top of a pitcher plant.
Soon, it will slide down inside and drown.

Some kinds of pitcher plants grow to be more than three feet (1 m) tall.

It lands on the edge of the plant and tries to suck up the liquid. But the sides of the leaves are steep and slippery. The insect slips and slides down them. At the bottom of the

pitcher is a liquid that the plant makes. The
insect falls into the liquid and drowns. The
plant digests the soft parts of the insect.
Only its skeleton is left.

Sundew Plants

Sundew plants trap insects on their sticky leaves. The leaves are covered in fine hairs. Each hair has a drop of sticky liquid at its red tip. The drops gleam in the sunlight like morning dew. That's where the name of this plant comes from.

The sundew plant is used as flypaper in some parts of the world.

A mosquito lands
on a sundew plant.

The hairs of a sundew plant bend over to trap an insect.

When an insect lands on a leaf, it sticks to a hair or two. It struggles to free itself, touching more sticky hairs. The nearby hairs bend over the insect and hold it down.

Once an insect is caught, the plant produces a juice. It pours this juice over the

insect. The juice turns the insect into a soup.
The plant eats the soup.

Sundew plants never pour their juices
onto anything but food. If a piece of sand
lands on a leaf, the plant will not produce
any juice.

Pretty but poisonous, eating any part of the lily of the valley plant will make you sick.

Chapter 2

Poisonous Plants

Unlike meat-eating plants, poisonous plants can hurt or even kill people. These plants make poisons to stop their enemies from eating them. Anything that eats these plants will become sick and may die.

Most poisonous plants taste bitter. The bitter taste keeps animals from eating these plants. Like you, most animals don't like bitter foods.

▶ Eating one leaf from this common houseplant could kill you.

Some poisonous plants use chemicals to keep their enemies away. These plants sting any animal that brushes by them. If you brush against some of these plants, you may get a painful rash. Other poisonous plants will actually prick you with their poison. They work like a doctor's needle.

The poisons in a henbane plant can cause seizures.

The monkshood plant is one of the most dangerous poisonous plants. Tiny amounts of its poison can kill.

Did You Know?

Hundreds of years ago in Italy, murderers gave their victims gloves dusted with a poison made from the monkshood plant. The poison entered the victim's body through cuts or scratches on his or her fingers.

Poison ivy can make you break out in an itchy rash.

Poison Ivy

"Leaves in three, let them be." Remember this saying. It's a reminder to stay away from a common poisonous plant: poison ivy. These three-leaf plants grow as climbing vines or low plants. They often grow along the side of roads or next to forest paths.

When you're out on a hike, look out for these shiny, pointed leaves. They contain a sticky oil. If you brush against them, the oil gets on your skin. You might feel the sting right away. Or your skin might start to itch like crazy a few hours later. Ugly, red blisters will appear. The rash can last for weeks. Don't scratch! You'll only spread the rash.

You can get a rash from poison ivy even if you never touch the plant. People can get it by touching animals that have brushed against these plants. The ivy's oil can even be spread by garden tools, picnic things, or anything that has touched the plants.

Stinging Nettles

Other poisonous plants have weaker chemicals but a stronger sting. Their poisons don't just ooze out. These plants put their poisons right into the skin of any creature that comes near.

The leaves of the stinging nettle are covered with millions of tiny, hollow spikes. The spikes are filled with acid. The tips of the spikes break off when they are touched. What is left of the spike is very sharp.

If you happen to brush by a stinging nettle, its spikes will cut your skin. Then, acid will flow into the cut and you'll get a hot, painful rash. Usually, the rash will go away after an hour or two. But some people suffer for a day or more.

Did You Know?

People use stinging nettle to treat joint pain. Chemicals in the nettles reduce inflammation in the body.

Stinging nettles grow in temperate climates.

Chapter 3

Amazing Plants

Plants really are amazing. The plants you have been reading about have developed special ways to survive. They have found ways to protect themselves from their enemies and to find food.

Scientists continue to discover new facts about plants. They know that some plants can help fight disease. These plants are used to make medicines. So far, scientists have studied only a tiny number of all flowering plants. We can only guess what amazing facts about plants they will find next.

Despite being poisonous, foxglove is used to make medicine.

How to Write an A+ Report

1. Choose a topic.

- Find something that interests you.
- Make sure it is not too big or too small.

2. Find sources.

- Ask your librarian for help.
- Use many different sources: books, magazine articles, and websites.

3. Gather information.

- Take notes. Write down the big ideas and interesting details.
- Use your own words.

4. Organize information.

- Sort your notes into groups that make sense.

- Make an outline. Put your groups of notes in the order you want to write your report.

5. Write your report.

- Write an introduction that tells what the report is about.

- Use your outline and notes as you write to make sure you say everything you want to say in the order you want to say it.

- Write an ending that tells about your report.

- Write a title.

6. Revise and edit your report.

- Read your report to make sure it makes sense.

- Read it again to check spelling, punctuation, and grammar.

7. Hand in your report!

Glossary

acid	a chemical substance that can burn your skin
adapt	to change to fit new conditions
bait	something used to attract another animal
bitter	an unpleasant taste that is strong and harsh
digest	to break down food into a form the body can use
dissolve	to mix into a liquid
inflammation	swelling caused by an infection or injury
microscope	a tool used to look at very small objects
mineral	an element needed by plants and animals
ooze	to leak out slowly
poison	a substance that can make you ill
protect	to keep safe
rash	an irritation of the skin
skeleton	the bones of an animal
survive	to keep living
trigger	something that causes something else to happen

Further Reading

• Books •

Aaseng, Nathan. *Meat-Eating Plants (Weird and Wacky)*. Berkeley Heights, NJ: Enslow Publishers, 1996. Ages 9-12, 48 pages.

Ballard, Carol. *Flowers (Variety of Life)*. Milwaukee, WI: Gareth Stevens Publishing, 2005. Ages 9-12, 32 pages.

Halfmann, Janet. *Plant Tricksters (Watts Library)*. London: Franklin Watts, 2004. Ages 9-12, 64 pages.

Hardwood, Penny. *Meat-Eating Plants (Eye View)*. New York, NY: Peter Bedrick, 2003. Ages 9-12, 32 pages.

Kneidel, Sally. *Skunk Cabbage, Sundew Plants, and Strangler Figs: And 18 More of the Strangest Plants on Earth*. Hoboken, NJ: John Wiley & Sons, 2001. Ages 9-12, 124 pages.

Richardson, Joy. *The Search for Cures From the Rain Forest (Science Quest)*. Milwaukee, WI: Gareth Stevens Publishing, 2005. Ages 9-12, 32 pages.

Souza, D.M. *Meat-Eating Plants (Watts Library)*. London: Franklin Watts, 2002. Ages 9-12, 64 pages.

• Websites •

ARKive: Images of Life on Earth
http://www.arkive.org/

Botanical Society of America
http://www.botany.org/
Carnivorous_Plants/

Fact monster
http://www.factmonster.com/
ipka/A0932475.html

Hawaiian Botanicals Inc.
http://www.hawaiianbotanicals.
com/cpintro.html

Museum of Unnatural Mystery
http://www.unmuseum.org/
maneatp.htm

ThinkQuest
http://library.thinkquest.org/
C007974/

Index